# RED TO BLACK

—

The Art of the Corporate Turnaround

PERRY M.
**ANDERSON**

## Legal Notices

# Dedication

*This book is dedicated to all the entrepreneurs and business owners who have put in the innumerable hours and wrestled with the challenging questions in order to see their dreams materialize. I am inspired by your determination to make your part of the world a better place.*

*This book is also dedicated to my father, J. Gunnar Anderson...the smartest man I know.*

# Table of Contents

# Foreword

The economies of Europe and North America (at least) are three quarters made up of small independent business - those with typically less than 250 people. And yet, the media is dominated by glamourous names, the largest few hundred corporations that in fact make up only a tiny proportion of the total economy. These very large companies demand preferential access to the best professional support services and cheap financing. Their problems are attended to by sympathetic regulators and they use their sheer scale to leverage economic and legal advantages over their smaller competitors.

Our passion is around levelling the playing field to correct these competitive disadvantages: helping the smaller business community flourish and bring enormous corresponding benefits to the overall economy. It was in such mutual efforts that I first met Perry Anderson. Perry is a very clever and passionate supporter of small-to-medium sized enterprise. In writing this book, he acknowledges the fact that most small businesses will face a financial crisis at some point in their lifecycle.

Within this book, Perry addresses the broader brushstrokes of bringing a business back from the brink of bankruptcy. While practical solutions deal with the immediate crisis, Perry then offers some highly innovative solutions which will also place the business on a stronger platform for the future. One such solution features the often-overlooked advantage small businesses possess in that they are able to function more like a team working toward a common purpose. This partnership approach provides unexpected commercial and financial benefits in addition to the obvious cultural advantages.

Perry's enthusiasm and experience shows through the following pages. I do hope and expect that this book will help you to transform your business.

**David Hart**

*Founder of Optimal Compliance*
**www.optimalcompliance.com**

---

David Hart trained as a Chartered Accountant and Chartered Tax Adviser with PwC in London, going on to run the most profitable Corporate Tax group in the PwC firm. He set up a small software business which is now a public company valued at around £85MM as well the Optimal Compliance consultancy which helps small businesses with structure, culture, tax, legal and accounting strategy and management.

# Introduction

If you are holding this book, you may be considering the need to turn a business around - maybe even your own. Perhaps the letters of demands for payment and the threats of lawsuits are already on your desk. The questions running through your mind are along the lines of *How bad is it really? Can we make it? Is it too late?*

If you are in the red and creditor calls are coming in daily, what you hold in your hand is the solution to your problems.

From nearly two decades of work in the Private Equity industry, I am convinced that businesses are closing up when it is not necessary. Things may be dark, to be sure, but I believe many small- to medium-sized businesses could benefit from options that are not widely known. My team and I have facilitated and been a part of numerous business rescues and turnaround situations. I am continually entranced by the many ways creative, win-win solutions can be generated to stop the bleeding and vastly improve the financial health of an insolvent company.

Some of the advice in these pages is common sense wisdom regarding how to increase revenue and cut costs. On the other hand, some of the advice is lesser known and typically considered as options only for mega companies that generate billions in revenue. Regardless of the advice or actual strategy deployed, all of the options require a tenacious deep dive into operations and shrewd decision-making, in the face of complex questions and intense pressure.

Considering that much of corporate turnaround is well-addressed elsewhere, I wrote this book to provide a bird's eye view of what actually can be done until the conventional wisdom is exhausted and conclusive decisions must be made. I draw generalizations on business smarts that apply around the world, with particulars that are to be addressed according to local law. The information is presented for readers in the United Kingdom, the United States, and Canada. Where there are significant differences, I bring them up in enough detail so you can investigate specifics with your local professionals.

In the concluding two rescue options, 1) the Limited Liability Partnership (LLP) and 2) the Company Voluntary Arrangement (CVA), or Chapter 11 Reorganization, I draw a more complete sketch of the processes, yet maintain a broad enough level so readers from various nations will not get lost in nuances that do not apply. At any rate, the information is meant to reveal the possibilities and encourage the pursuit of highly qualified local insolvency practitioners and turnaround consultants, not give step by step instructions. Readers who are not from the countries I focus on should be able to find enough information in order to undertake the equivalent actions in their own jurisdictions.

If you are pondering the possibility that your company is insolvent, this book will provide new information to consider. It is a quick read. It will help you know if you should close up shop or if you can save the company. As you know, time is of the essence. I encourage you to read with an open mind and with hope.

Bankruptcy is not necessarily inevitable.

## CHAPTER 1

# Are We Insolvent?

**Chapter Summary** *Three basic tests will tell a troubled Director, CEO, or manager if their company is at the brink of insolvency: The Cash Flow Test, the Balance Sheet Test, and the Legal Test.*

———

Directors and CEOs tell me that they began to wonder exactly how much trouble their company was in when they could no longer deny that a few specific scenarios indicated trouble:

> *The same week I got a refusal of credit from the bank we've dealt with for decades. That shook me. Then our main sheet metal vendor, the CFO, a good friend of mine, called and lost it and started shouting that they were done with us. They'd lost a big order that our payment was to have made happen.*

> *I'd quit taking a paycheck maybe five months before that, but one afternoon the controller stayed late, which she never did, and slipped into my office after everyone was gone and whispered to me, the tears just rolling down her face, that she just couldn't get the numbers to produce payroll in two days.*

> *I realized, one night after that one awful day, that all I was doing any more was playing fireman. Putting out fires. Not managing a thriving*

*business. All these problems, and always they got back to money. That put a sick feeling in my gut that didn't go away for six months.*

*Statutory demand. I thought we'd been doing pretty good keeping things running until we had three weeks to come up with $245,000.*

No business owner or manager wants to face the possibility of insolvency and all that it implies. However, when the big picture solidifies, denial no longer serves. You are going to have to look closely at the facts to decide if your company is insolvent.

Three simple tests will show if your company is insolvent. You may even know the answers to these questions without having to go look for concrete numbers.

## Cash Flow Test

Can the company pay its debts when they fall due? The two most obvious places to look are employer-paid portions of income taxes and payroll deductions, and the span of time it takes you to pay your vendors.

First, are you on time paying employer-submitted portions of national and local income taxes plus other mandatory payroll deductions like health care, disability, and survivor benefits? Even if you are making payments on time at this moment in time, if you have been in arrears, are you paying enough to catch up in a timely manner?

Second, are you paying your suppliers on their desired terms? If they invoice at Net 30, but you regularly pay Net 60 or Net 90, this is a sign of trouble. It may simply be that your controller is a bit stingy and prefers to hang onto every cent as long as possible, but maybe not!

The cash flow test is pretty straightforward and cannot be faked. Either you are paying your bills or you are not. In the event you have not been making payroll, your bank, vendors, and employees will let you know.

## Balance Sheet Test

Does the company owe more in liabilities than the reasonable market value of held assets? Many directors will look at their balance sheets and decide that the company is solvent. However, scrutiny may reveal overstatements like stock that is obsolete or low in realized value, mis-categorizations of work-in-progress, or accounts receivables that are not expected or actually collectible. Dilapidation and depreciation are easy to overlook or miscalculate, but these errors also skew the true picture.

Certain line items may be missing entirely, such as contingent or prospective liabilities. For instance, if there is a pending legal ruling to formally determine how much the company owes, this should be calculated in the balance sheet.

Proper accounting and up-to-date numbers may bring the balance sheets to show insolvency.

## The Legal Test

Has a creditor obtained a judgment against the company? The final and most decisive indicator is whether there is any kind of legal ruling against the company.

If a creditor issues a statutory demand or involuntary petition for an amount over a particular figure, you have a set number of days, depending on the laws where your company is located, to pay that amount or come to repayment terms with your creditor. If you fail to meet the creditor's demands, the creditor is within rights to begin liquidation and wind up proceedings. In fact, any demand for payment that you do not dispute makes the company fair game for proceedings, regardless of whether any legal claims are first issued.

———

The truth is that as Director or CEO, you should know how bad things are. By law, it is your direct responsibility to have an accurate grasp of your bottom line - how things stand with your suppliers or creditors, and what kinds of demands your accountant is fielding.

Now, if accounts reflecting the most accurate picture of the company's financial status show insufficient cash to pay liabilities on time, you - the CEO and Board of Directors - must take immediate action to address the situation.

# CHAPTER 2

# How Did We End Up Facing Insolvency?

**Chapter Summary** *A number of factors contribute to corporate insolvency, with varying degrees in each instance. Ongoing situations like poor accounting, poor systems, and poor decision-making can be avoided. Other factors, like lawsuits and rising costs, cannot always be anticipated early enough to offset the impact.*

---

A variety of statistics are floating around regarding small business failure rates. The Small Business Administration (SBA) Office of Advocacy website indicates that while about 80% of small businesses will survive the first year, the odds decline sharply after that. At the five-year mark, 45% - 51% remain open. About 33% of small businesses remain viable at 10 years.[1]

If you keep looking, all of the statistics conflict with one another to some degree, and many of them read dismally. However, running a business is simply a series of risks day in and day out. There are many ways one can define business success or failure, and statistics eventually cease to be helpful. The final analysis comes down to whether you can continue to bring your products and services to market.

Solvency depends on two elements: correct knowledge and sufficient resources. Lack of right knowledge tends to manifest as a slow and difficult downward spiral. Many business leaders know they have problems, but they either fail to take them seriously enough, or they do not find the right solutions. Solvency also requires sufficient resources. Insufficient resources may be caused by lack of understanding but may also be due to reasons beyond company control: market shifts, rising vendor costs, the fallout from legislation and governmental directives, or lawsuits.

In the first category, I encounter three types of lack of knowledge: poor accounting, poor decision making, and inadequate systems, or some combination thereof.

## Poor Accounting

**Lack of proper business practices.** Some business practices are the same across industries. For example, accounting and contracts are universal. Passion for the product or service, even a blockbuster offering, is no substitute for a foundation of solid business practices. Not understanding every clause in a contract you enter into might turn out to be a fatal mistake. Poor accounting can cause problems such as ineffective budgeting, unsustainable debt service or cash flow, tax issues, possibly even unintentional fraud.

**Not understanding financial statements.** Directors can possess excellent leadership skills, yet not have a complete command of the balance sheet. Be sure that you and your board understand the balance sheet and all its implications because when you begin to make decisions based on incomplete understanding, trouble will follow.

**Inaccurately or poorly prepared financial statements.** Recall the Balance Sheet Test to measure insolvency. A closer look at a company's spreadsheet can reveal subtle misallocations such as work-in-progress or old inventory at inflated values. It is incumbent upon the CEO and the financial officer to be sure that the controller or accountant clearly understands correct allocations per your industry, including current valuations. This includes correct programming of accounting software and proper updates.

**Inaccurate cost accounting.** If you cannot state which of your services or products are contributing to the bottom line and which are subtracting from it, and if you do not identify where prices need to be adjusted and costs trimmed, you can easily find yourself in trouble. Fixed and variable costs need to be checked regularly, and appropriate adjustments made when the margins grow too thin.

## Poor Systems

**Lack of expense control.** Any company, healthy or not, must keep an eye on expenses, measuring return for the investment. Company cars, advertising, and equipment are common areas where businesses overspend. Revisit the department budgets carefully and realistically, putting measures in place so managers and employees cannot spend unnecessarily.

**Outdated industry protocol.** It worked well for a time, but the technology and equipment in use twenty or even two years ago probably no longer serves you. Along with new technology and equipment come new processes, new decision trees, and applications of new industry developments. Someone in the company needs to be on top of industry trends. You may not be able to respond to every variation, but some will come along that you simply - literally - cannot afford to let pass. If you regularly experience computer, phone or internet lag or downtime, or if you cannot comply with required vendor applications, it is past time to upgrade your hardware and/or software.

**Unclear company organization.** For every activity that must be undertaken, anyone in the company should be able to point to the person responsible for its execution - from compliance with regulations to taking out the trash. If someone is always having to step in at the last second to take care of issues that should have been routine, the board needs to revisit the organizational chart and duty assignments.

## Poor Decision Making

**Lack of sensitivity to market.** As with outdated industry protocol, management needs to be aware of what might soon or is now impacting consumer response. Depending on your industry, anything from pending legislation to natural disasters overseas can drive consumer behaviour or your own ability to produce. Technological developments and the competition's activity need to be in the corner of your eye all the time. Prognostication is admittedly a skill not everyone can develop. However, paying attention and asking thoughtful questions is far more likely to put you in a position of anticipation rather than keeping your head down.

**Inept personnel.** Some of the harder decisions I have seen company directors face have been around particular employees who remain on the payroll but are not worth the trouble they create. Misplaced loyalty can drain department budgets, cause ill will with other staff members and customers, and ultimately spell the doom of the company. I do not pretend to have answers for situations when these directors rationalize retention of their problem employee, but my sympathy wanes when situations that otherwise would have been reversible continue to worsen after a disruptive, non-contributing, or otherwise inept individual is allowed to remain.

**Keeping customers that cost more than they bring in.** Some customers and clients consume time that is not compensated, damage company morale by being difficult to work with, or negotiate prices that do not cover costs. These clients should not be maintained simply for the potential revenue. Find a kind but firm way to invite them to step up or take their business elsewhere.

## Situations Far Less Controllable by the Company

**Lawsuits and payouts.** Some lawsuits from customers, competitors, or other associates can be anticipated, but some come from out of the blue. Significant judgments against you may be large enough to bring operations to a halt. The resulting cessation of income leads to unpaid bills and creditors.

**Rising vendor costs.** Many owners try for as long as they can to avoid passing their own rising costs on to their customers and clients. Prices for raw goods and transportation increase relentlessly. Governmental policies for safety and environmental concerns add to expenses with little to no recognizable return. Businesses that rely on overseas trade have the potential of being crippled by tariffs overnight.

——

Even when you see them coming, some situations just will not have easy answers. They will be very messy when they have been allowed to develop over years. However, you must act - you must do your best to make decisions that will protect cash flow.

Making a decision and knowing what to do, of course, must be followed by action. Sometimes it is the company leadership itself that is paralyzed, for a variety of reasons, and so the company circles the drain.

In every corporate turnaround situation I have encountered, tough decisions must be made. I have worked with CEOs who are very committed to saving the company until it comes down to that one critical decision - acting on that one decision. Had it been made months or years ago, acting on that single point may have saved a great deal of grief for everyone involved.

A couple times, action was not taken, and the whole recovery effort was for naught. I say this to make it very clear that proper knowledge is necessary and beneficial, but it is not the only factor in turning around a distressed company. In addition to doing a lot of hard professional work to save your career, reputation, and the livelihoods of those around you, you - as the director - may be required to take a hard look within.

## CHAPTER 3
# What Should We Do?

**Chapter Summary** *Insolvency always has to do with cash flow, so the places that cash flow stops are the places to address in avoiding bankruptcy proceedings. Some options will result in immediate changes to the balance sheet, while others take more time.*

———

It always has to do with cash flow.

Too little cash available versus too many bills is the reason companies get into trouble. This is basic enough logic, so the first solutions that managers and directors think of involve putting more cash in the asset column and less in the liability column. They do what they can to increase revenues, cut costs, and save every possible penny.

Prices are nudged upward. New products or services are added to the line-up.

Non-vital allocations are slashed or frozen.

Employees are given fewer hours or are let go altogether, or their classifications are changed so that they are not eligible for benefits or overtime.

Requests for software updates and equipment repair are denied.

These strategies work - for a while. However, they usually end up creating other problems.

Expendable employees were made redundant, but other key staff members became stretched too thin trying to make up the difference…and they quit. Non-essential repair and upgrades were put off, but now production is behind because of unsupported software and undependable machinery.

Eventually, the realization will be that these kinds of measures simply cannot return enough savings to save the company - not in a month…and not in six months.

And if the creditors are starting to get more forceful when they call, you are out of time. If a creditor has filed for winding up (starting the process of dissolving a company) against you, you certainly do not have six months. Depending on local laws, you may have a matter of days to come by enough cash to convince your creditors their money is safe.

**66**

Is it possible to turn a business around inside a week?

## Success is not final, failure is not fatal: it is the courage to continue that counts.

~ *Winston Churchill*

Yes, it is.

You have to take extreme actions - digging much deeper than the obvious firing and slashing described above. You will have to reject any pride that has kept you from acknowledging that there was a problem long ago. You will have to uncover unsavoury realities about the business that might have saved you sooner had you looked closer. If you do not want the doors to close, you and your managers will have to find new levels of trust, cooperation, and determination.

———

The following chapters take a look at the five most common strategies to undertake when the books begin to show an alarming amount of red. Some strategies you have already tried and some are a more thorough version of what you have already tried. Some ideas will contradict others. The ultimate decisions and tactics will have to make sense for your situation, depending on factors to which only you can speak.

## Other Things to Know: Dealing with Creditors

*While you are still going over your options and making your decisions, you will likely still have creditors calling and knocking, wanting their money. Do what you can to remain business-like, no matter the scenarios that are running through your mind. Keeping a level head during dealings at this point will only serve you favourably, no matter your ultimate decision.*

— Know your debt amount and repayment terms to each creditor, and the rights they have. Have your accountant pull together a quick reference chart, including contact information.

— Identify the real decision-maker at every organization, and deal with them, if possible.

— Communicate with every creditor calmly.

— Do not refuse calls or neglect to return calls, as this will only increase their suspicions that you are in trouble and may hasten their petition against you.

— Acknowledge trouble and be ready to give a brief outline of what you are doing to repay obligations. Do not promise anything except to keep them informed. Do what you can to build their trust.

— Get every agreement in writing. Keep notes of every conversation including when, to whom you spoke, and other details. It may be a good idea to record conversations but be careful of doing so without consent.

# CHAPTER 4
# Solution #1: Increase Revenue

**Chapter Summary** *Increasing revenue is the most obvious first step in stemming the cash haemorrhage. Some efforts will produce immediate revenues, and others will take a little more time. Tactics in sales, accounts receivable, and accounting in general should result in a fair boost of income.*

———

As you know, increasing revenue is the most obvious place to start to increase cash flow. Even when this was done well and to good immediate effect, there are many other detailed ways companies can fine-tune the income engine for greater efficiency.

Depending on your particular situation, some of these tactics will produce a difference in the bottom line within a day or two, while other efforts will take a longer time to reap the benefits. Work with your board and staff to triage your time and efforts to the most productive manoeuvres, understanding that you will have to come back with deeper audits later.

## Immediate Revenue

If you have not already, the easiest step is to raise your prices. It is easy to talk yourself out of raising prices. Fear of losing customers is a primary reason that business leaders decide not to raise their prices. Even when faced with their own rising overhead and production costs, they reason that their customers' expenses are going up too, and they do not want to be the bad guy, especially if they are the first locally in the industry to raise prices. However, this is a poor rationalization when considering the livelihoods of employees, who will have a tough time coping with the rising cost of living without a job. At the end of the day, a 10% increase in prices across the board annually is not unreasonable in today's economy, especially if your competitors have already raised their prices.

Assuming your cash flow projections are accurate, take a second to run the maths on a 5% or 10% price increase. I have seen some models that can return as much as 40%. Bottom line, raising your prices is an increase in your instantly accessible cash flow. Remember, you are trying to keep your doors open.

In addition to this step consider the impact of these strategies:

— **Have a major sale event. This could be a limited-time discount for new offerings or upgrades for your best customers or for leads you have been nurturing. Have a fire sale to clear out old and slow-moving inventory. To execute this quickly, notify your customers with an email or social media blast directed to decision-makers. Do not take the time to draft a mailer. If you are not already bombarding your client list with sale offers, this can pique quite a bit of interest.**

— **Create up-sell and cross-sell tactics. For example,** *Buy a year's worth of product/service now and receive a 10% discount*, **or 10% discount for payment in advance. This brings in a year's worth of revenue that would otherwise be trickling in over time. Again, draft the sale parameters and direct your sales staff to contact your clients or customers via phone, email, or other social media tools.**

— **Add to your distribution platforms. For example, instead of selling only on Amazon, find other online channels. Some customers are extremely loyal to one online retailer, and even though you provide exactly what they are looking for, they will never find you because you are not where they are.**

— **If you have the option, and it makes sense in other ways, consider a retail offering if you sell wholesale. This may work better for boutique type goods and service. Conversely, consider a wholesale** offering if your goods can be provided in bulk. Wholesalers often buy in bulk and frequently have established transportation networks, which you can leverage to reduce costs.

— Contact your current customers about upgrades. Judiciously offer discounts, immediate delivery, or other such enticements.

— Take a look at open orders. There may be ways to hurry the invoicing process a bit, perhaps via phone calls, to see that orders have been delivered, or checking if there were any issues with the order that are delaying conversion to invoice.

## Brainstorm Other Creative Selling Tactics

Once you have executed what you can for immediate turnaround, gather your staff and brainstorm other tactics you can unroll over a week or a month. Use these ideas to jump start your list of possibilities.

— Remember your current loyal customers, the clients or customers on your working 'hot leads' list, former customers who drifted away unnoticed, or old leads who may be enticed with new offerings. Find a way to engage each list.

— If you do not have such options already, consider creating two or three tiers of products or services, or a handful of packages. Re-contact non-buyers to see if a different value level would have more appeal.

— Launch a new offering if you have one in the offing. Make sure you have completed and double checked all due diligence, and do not undertake this if there is any chance it will not be well-received by the market, or if it will not realistically provide revenue within the timeframe that you need it.

— Current clients may be willing to give a set number of references in exchange for an incentive like a discount or favourable contract extension.

— A friendly competitor might be interested in exchanging lost leads lists, or the owners of a business in a complementary market might be persuaded to exchange mailing lists.

# Boost Accounts Receivable

Set your sales staff up to keep the phone lines and social media outlets busy, then head into the billing department and spend some time in accounts receivables. Inspect both open and recently closed invoices, and you are likely to find a number of revenue leaks. Companies can lose upwards of 7% of their revenue through oversights in the asset accounts. Proper corrections here can significantly change the numbers on the balance sheet.

Check line items versus invoices, RFPs versus sales orders, and vendor order acknowledgments against POs. If it is possible, having fresh eyes go over these orders may be best to identify errors and inconsistencies. Again, go line item by line item against the correct price lists, proper billing procedures, and timelines. Look for

- **Missed billing**
- **Un-invoiced work done outside of warranty or work not detailed in the contracted scope of work**
- **Unpaid and past-due customer invoices**
- **Uncollected expenses or client reimbursements**
- **Out of date price lists being used. Check every single department that has the ability to set customer prices and ensure that everyone is using the right pricing.**
- **Delay of contract renewal. Renewal should be initiated and in place before the current contract runs out.**
- **Invoices not reliably being raised in a timely manner**

## Additional Accounting Efforts

When the pressure is off a little, spend more time seeking other ways to increase revenue or limit revenue leakage in the daily operations.

- **Examine all open orders or unfulfilled sales orders and find out why they have not been fulfilled yet. While taking care that no other problems are created, implement changes in the process to complete the ones that can be billed upon as soon as possible.**
- **Consider software options that will allow your clients and customers to pay online, rather than dealing with paper, stamps,**

and postal carrier delays. **This will increase your revenue more quickly.**

— Discounting should be done only by senior sales staff at extreme or planned discretion or done by sales software that cannot be edited. Do not allow sales reps their own discretion in discounts.

— Any coupons offered should expire quickly and be tracked to be sure they are applied properly. Likewise, referral codes should be limited in time and number and made non-transferrable.

— Revaluate your refund policy. Tighten it if necessary and establish assurances against fraudulent refunds.

— Review your customer service to ensure that policy and staffing is sufficient to prevent chargebacks. The review should include contract wording, pertinent instructions, proof of delivery, consistent policy for resolution of issues, and so on.

## The Accounting Software

Software designers are always working to create stop-gaps against errors and miscalculations in their programs; the best ones request feedback and maintain customer service. Notwithstanding, the possibility exists that error is built in. Run some of the maths by hand if you begin to see something consistently amiss.

## You got to choose between tightening your belt or losing your pants.

~ *Navjot Singh Sidhu*

Along this same line, when things have stabilized, contact your accounting software company and be sure that you have received all the appropriate software updates and bug fixes. It may be time to evaluate your accounting package altogether, if you find that your staff has developed work arounds to accommodate an unsolved issue, a consistent glitch that the software firm does not acknowledge, or anything else that hampers automated efficiency.

If the business is going to stay open, it may be a good idea to have a formal accounting audit to investigate the true usefulness of your current software, the skill and work division of your accounting staff, workflow needs, *etc.* Effective staff allocation and priority of billing processes can make your accounts receivable hum right along, an asset to a thriving company.

To recap, the above tactics should be put into practice immediately. These efforts will take considerable effort from you, your board and your senior staff. However, you should see a surge of revenue within a couple of days. It may be enough to satisfy your creditors that you are serious about staying in business and working with them to mutual satisfaction.

## CHAPTER 5

# Solution #2: Cut Costs

**Chapter Summary** *In addition to increasing revenue, cost-cutting measures can also be implemented. Savings - less cash flowing out the door - can be realized in current open orders, in purchasing, and in in-house processes.*

———

Along with increasing revenue, the most obvious step to take in boosting cash flow is cutting costs. Deloitte found that 74% of CPOs make cost reduction one of the central pillars of their business strategies.[2] As stated before, some of these efforts will see differences in the balance sheet within 24 - 48 hours of hard work, others will manifest a difference later. Determine what will shift the balance sheet most significantly for your situation, and what will have to be worked out when creditors are satisfied that you are committed to honouring your commitments to them.

## Savings in Current Orders

For potentially quick results, spend time combing through recent and current purchase orders. Trace through billing, payments, discounts, transportation, inventory, and so on, ensuring that every discount and allowance is accounted for. You may find recoverable leakages here and there in the shape of missed discounts or calculation errors.

- Double check that accurate orders are being placed and what you order is being shipped.
- Ensure that you are paying only for what has been ordered. Document the payment and delivery terms and the quality of the product received. Take nothing for granted.
- Make sure you are receiving agreed upon discounts on every invoice. Human error or software error can occur.
- Apply newly negotiated terms to open orders, if permitted.

## Savings in Procurement

The purchase of the goods and services you need to provide your own products or services is where the majority of your ongoing costs accrue. Strategic restructuring of your procurement practices can go a long way to reduce your outgoing cash flow.

When working with clients who are trying to salvage distressed businesses, I find it enlightening to do some simple maths around procurement practices. Managers admit that their purchasing strategy is based solely on economics: they purchase from whomever offers them the best price. However, when running the numbers on all the possibilities, we frequently find less obvious but more cost-effective decision trees. For example, it can be better to consolidate purchases from as few vendors as possible, negotiating bulk discounts. When bulk purchases can be effectively managed at the warehouse, this prevents leakage of cash for repeated transportation charges, while consolidated delivery will save time and cash as well.

Both improved purchase power and time savings increase cash flow. Greater predictability of the purchase cycle will enable you to identify bottlenecks or slow periods that can be dealt with in other ways.

Have a hard look at your purchasing processes and put all your options with every supplier and potential vendor on the table. Engage managers and top employees in procurement departments to be sure you understand why they do what they do, and why other things are not being done. There may be compelling reasons to do this versus that, but sometimes the only reason turns out to be 'We have always done it that way'. Spend time exhausting all possible scenarios and implement decisions that will reduce spending without causing other problems that nullify the savings.

- Revisit every single contract with every single vendor, checking for discounts and bulk purchase opportunities.

- Take advantage of annual or bulk discounts, rebates and other sensible incentives. Take care, though, that the warehouse has capacity to handle the volume - physically and electronically - without obstruction of other processes, or your savings will disappear into delays. Once the price adjustments are contracted, go into billing and sales - both personnel and software - to be sure that they are applied correctly to every purchase order going out and sales order coming back in.

- Examine all shipping options, taking into account inventory capacity. Mathematically, it might make the most sense to pay a little more for materials from a different vendor but reap much better savings on rail versus over-the-road transportation.

- Request a non-payment holiday from the vendors with whom you are still on good terms.

- If a contract is extremely oppressive, seek to be released from it.

Some of these negotiation points will depend of course where relationships stand with your creditors. Supposing that things have been amiable until now, your vendors are more likely to be open to negotiating in good faith. Negotiation may be trickier if distrust has been allowed to build up.

While a hard look at the whole purchasing process will end up being a longer process than can be completed in a few days, it is vitally important in the long run - and should yield some positive results in terms of keeping large amounts of cash from flowing away.

## Savings In-House

When you have exhausted all emergency measures, you will want to take time to challenge every point in procurement channels, whether raw materials or office supplies. Get details on paper. A visual flow chart may help you pinpoint gaps and leaks.

- Decide if you can or should eliminate goods or services that are not recouping production outlays. Do not forget that such steps may lead to cutting or re-defining certain job roles or marketing campaigns. Be sure you calculate these impacts correctly.

- Switch to vendors who are competitive and who will offer you a competitive edge. Changes in the economy, end user consumption patterns, and market volatility may be creating requirements that are different from two, five, or more years ago when the purchasing relationship was first made. If your supplier is not staying innovative themselves, they will be unable to offer you the best for your own clients and customers. Vendors who are consistently late, who communicate poorly, or who deliver damaged or subpar goods are adding to your troubles, not helping you, even if they discount. Look at your vendors' vendors to see if any advantageous relationships can be negotiated by going elsewhere on the distribution chain.

- Examine typical orders to see if a different spec or design might lower costs while remaining appropriate for the final use. Consult with suppliers, best customers, and professionals who may have better knowledge of what really drives costs. Be sure that you are not falling prey to brand loyalty or outdated information.

- Standardize as much as possible across your equipment, fleet, or other ways. For instance, provide only one make and model of vehicle for your sales staff so that lower inventory of parts is kept on hand for maintenance or repair.

- Bring external roles or operations inside, repositioning or training existing staff if necessary. An example would be building contractors handling their own concrete needs rather than subcontracting.

- Alternately, see what non-core activities you might be able to outsource, such as security, housekeeping, or information technology. Look for service specialists who have excellent reputations and will give you a probationary period.

- Sell equipment you have not used in a year, unless it is something you must have once a year and cannot rent it. This might mean part or all of the company fleet. In addition to gaining space, you will have the income from the sale, lowering your housing and maintenance overhead.

- When permitted, renegotiate your lease, or sublet unused building or yard space.

- Go over every insurance policy with your broker. First, be sure you are not paying for coverage you do not need. Then, be sure that your insurance needs are not extending beyond coverage if you shift things around internally.

- Ensure that unauthorized purchases are not being charged to accounts. Purchasing should be an efficient process with unalterable checks and balances. Emergency purchases should be vetted by a few authorized managers.
- Assuming you have not already, undertake an austerity audit. Every expense, down to the petty cash box, is suspect. If it can be quantified, it is subject to consideration. Again, think things through to be sure that a change here does not have a negative impact somewhere else that will directly affect production and delivery, and therefore cash flow.

Look for ways you might be practicing 'Penny wise but pound foolish'. Saving a penny per piece makes no sense if it takes a 25 minute phone call to place the order. Go with the supplier who gives you a one-click purchase. Make sure department heads are moving the company forward instead of managing petty issues.

As already mentioned, for some companies, a complete software overhaul may be necessary to streamline every accounting, purchasing, and inventory function. Automated billing can save on staff costs, and can give your customers a way to pay electronically. This will be a larger step to consider at a later point, but you should keep this strategy in mind when making decisions about how to move forward.

In the matter of firing the customers and clients whose business is no longer worth the fiscal and emotional cost they accrue, letting go of such customers must be handled with great delicacy these days. If you have such clients, you will have to weigh these scenarios as seriously as every other tactic I am describing. You would do well to consult your legal team as to the best way to send these clients on their way, or, at the very least, the ways that you should not do so.

---

In the end, the central question driving your supply management is, 'Do we really need this in order to do what we do?' Your answer needs to be educated and thoughtful, based on reliable employee observation and hard data, rather than guesswork and a quick 'Yes' or 'No'. Look at it through the lens of the Pareto Principle. When you suppose that 20% of your spending is done via established vendors with established purchasing systems, the remaining 80% of your purchasing is done without following any procurement policy. This is far too much outlay to leave to the whims of anyone who can justify 'just a laptop' or 'just a new drill press'.

The expenses of managing your procurement process should give you a significant return. Keep this in mind as you are doing the grueling work of audits and decision making.

## Other Things to Know:
## Fastest Cash Recoup Strategies

*As mentioned, time is of the essence once the statutory demand has reached you. Some of the stop-gap measures can be executed quickly in order to raise revenue, and results will take longer with other measures. You should see immediate relief from these efforts:*

### Increase revenue

— Raise prices across the board by 5% – 15%.

— Make collection calls on all past due accounts. Offer to send someone to pick up a check in person or offer a discount for an electronic funds transfer.

— Follow up with current pending orders.

— Apply up-sell and cross-sell strategies, with a focus on up-front payment.

— Offer a major sale event to undecided prospects.

— Hold a fire sale.

— Offer loyal clients an upgrade or a limited-time discount.

### Cutting costs

— Go over payable contracts to ensure you are not over-paying.

— Request payment holidays with amenable vendors.

— Negotiate better terms on oppressive contracts.

— Remove redundant tasks or underperforming employees.

— Consider elimination or delay of a service or product which will result in instant reduction of expenditure without crippling day-to-day revenue.

— Terminate marketing expenditures for which there is little or no return on investment.

— Suspend capital purchases, hiring, and non-essential expenses.

# CHAPTER 6

# Solution #3: Manage Working Capital

**Chapter Summary** *Management of working capital is the day to day job of the company directors. Those who do not have a deliberate system in place should begin by tracking their current cash conversion cycle at every single actionable point in the company, decide on the most advantageous changes to be made without causing other problems, and then plan and execute a reasonable rollout. Adjusting with feedback on a continual basis will keep working capital positive.*

———

Working capital is the measurement of a company's financial health - the difference between assets and liabilities. Working capital is the cash flow that the company maintains and draws on to pay overhead, purchase raw materials, make payroll, and cover unexpected costs. A number of company activities are reflected in the working capital ratio, including accounts payable and accounts receivable, inventory management, and debt management. Positive working capital means that a business has enough money to cover daily operational expenses as well as meet short-term debt, *i.e.* payments on credit to vendors.

Accurate accounting and effective management of working capital will give directors accurate snapshots of the company's ability to meet obligations at certain points into the future. Skilled administration of working capital will not only keep things humming along well, it can also boost revenue. However, inaccurate cost accounting or misallocation will give a skewed picture of a company's true condition.

## Five Steps to Correctly Manage Working Capital

Following are the basic steps to achieve a grasp of your working capital from which you can make best decisions. Please note that many of these concepts have already been touched upon in previous sections and may be re-addressed soon. The point is not so much to bewilder an already overwhelmed director but to drive home the point that company survival depends on an intensive overhaul from top to bottom. You may find yourself circling back around, once stability is achieved by the short-term recovery efforts, to departments and systems you thought you had thoroughly investigated. In reality, there are multiple perspectives from which to examine every process and piece of data, so the more times you get fresh viewpoints on something, the better chance you have of making advantageous decisions.

Also note, you may find conflicting advice, for example, in the admonition to consider buying in bulk in order to take advantage of discounts versus the caution to maintain low inventory volume to keep cash from being tied up on the shelves for a period of time. In every instance, you will have to decide what is most expedient for your position. Even your closest competitor down the road will have an entirely different set of factors to account for in answering the same questions. Take advice, yes, but the ultimate decision will have to be your own.

### Step One - Measure

You must start with raw data - a baseline measurement of your current situation - in order to make and effect any decisions. Observe your cash conversion cycle - that is, the amount of time it takes for your cash to cycle through purchase into inventory, accounts payable, sales, and accounts receivable, and then back into cash. The quicker, the better.

Every industry will have a particular cycle, and your cycle will look different from everyone else in your industry. Therefore, while looking to see what needs to be changed to match best industry practices, you must always consider what will be the most effective scenario within your own walls. If you have only been guessing until now, find out what the current best practices are for your industry.

Ask your staff for deep enough levels of data to identify the patterns that emerge from the rotations of liability and asset. You may have to give them time to come up with the metrics you want. These include both the higher-level key performance indicators (KPIs) that you have always looked at, as well as those per each department: sales, marketing, factory floor, warehouse, accounting, and so on through the entire business. Dive as deeply as you must to understand why the numbers are what they are. In other words, do not look only at delivery time averages, examine them by customer type or product type and chase back to the factors in the process that influence each point. The low-level Key Performance Indicators (KPIs) are probably the numbers that will give you the most actionable figures at this point.

Look for any spots where cash gets stuck, such as clients who pay 60 or 90 days out, delayed invoicing, delayed delivery, bottlenecks in the production lines, consistent or significant customer service issues - anything that slows the production, delivery, and payment of your goods or services. The metrics from a single cycle will be instructive. A second cycle more so, and by the time you reach a third cycle, you will see clearly where things must change.

If possible, collect 12 months' projections. Doing so may be critical for identifying in advance any ebbs or flows of the cash flow significant enough to require carrying over.

## Step Two - Decide

Once you have good numbers assembled, meet with your managers and supervisors to pinpoint changes that can be made. Here are some examples of changes in various departments:

### In sales

- **Speed the sale completion loop to reduce inventory-carrying costs and avoid loss of revenue due to lost or delayed sales.**
- **Ensure that current pricing lists are in hand and that old price lists are unavailable. This includes prices input into your sales and accounting databases.**
- **Develop and enable responsive customer service to reduce customer dissatisfaction, while safeguarding against fraudulent returns or refunds.**

## In procurement

— Order locally to shorten procurement time and decrease inventory burden.

— Automate the ordering process to save time lost in procurement and mis-ordering.

— Reduce lead-time between ordering and receiving raw goods by revisiting vendor contracts and spelling out terms for lead-time.

## In production

— Upgrade software and machinery to avoid loss due to down time.

— Audit to be sure your software and equipment are indeed adequate for your goals, even if they are up-to-date and running well.

— Consider outsourcing for portions of the cycle.

— Work to find the sweet spot between cash tied up in slow-moving on-hand inventory and fulfilment delays due to waiting for delivery.

## In Accounts Payable

— Implement appropriate electronic payment methods which are less labour intensive and not susceptible to loss in the mail.

— Provide decision-making powers to those responsible for transactions to save processing time.

— Upgrading the AP process to electronic format as opposed to paper checks and billing will vastly increase efficiency plus reduce the possibility of error.

— Paying bills early can enhance your reputation as a high-value customer, netting you better service and prices.

## In Accounts Receivable

— Establish or re-establish billing procedures to eliminate delay. Use automated reminders.

— Eliminate or limit customers who carry too much credit. If necessary, hire outside debt collections to reduce uncollectible liability.

— Offer cash discounts if invoices are paid before the due date.

— Implement advance-pay incentives for customers, such as discounted or free product.

As mentioned before, these are only guides you should already have a good idea about. It is not an overstatement to say that absolutely every company activity should come under scrutiny.

In all cases, insist on full participation from every level of employee, and continue to practice accurate data collection to measure improvements. By this time, your staff should be very aware of why things are in upheaval. They will either be on-board in the interests of saving their jobs, or they should be shown the door. You cannot afford to keep employees who do not meet company standards and expectations.

## Step Three - Plan

Before you implement change, take a step back to consider the tiers of phases required for a successful overhaul rather than create descent into chaos. Some changes will need to be rolled out before others, and some can be implemented independently. Your plans in each department should be specific and measurable, with concrete dates and quantifiable accountability factors built in. Leave nothing to chance.

Get buy-in from your managers and supervisors, giving them time to prepare their workers appropriately for coming changes. Incentivizing strategies may be necessary or helpful in both the short term and the long term.

## Step Four - Implement

The only way you will experience a successful change of any size is through the full cooperation and participation of your staff. Once the changes are underway, keep the entire goal visible to everyone and remain open to feedback. Ensure that every step of every phase is being executed properly.

## Step Five - Adjust

Now is not the time to set and forget. Once your major implementations are in place, continue to measure and adjust according to expected and developing trends, both internal and external, foreseeable and unforeseen. Working capital management must be an ongoing effort.

———

The observations and decision-making of working capital management should be regular exercises for the C-suite and board. Leadership should seek accurate input from department heads who are also interested in the best advantages smart management has to offer. Regardless of what brought you to the brink of bankruptcy, the solutions lie in comprehensive and appropriate measures to create and maintain positive working capital.

## CHAPTER 7
# Solution #4: Revisit Marketing

**Chapter Summary** *Marketing seems like a mystery to many business leaders, but it should not. The first key is to obtain the services of a marketing professional with a proven track record of improved sales. A working understanding of available marketing tools and a crystal-clear picture of the ideal buyer are also essential for the best Return on Investment of marketing expenditures.*

It is common for directors and CEOs to find themselves in dire straits before finally admitting that their marketing is part of the problem. They know marketing is vitally important, but it can seem like a mysterious art that strategizes by guesswork or by throwing darts at a board full of ideas. Success may or may not follow, and if it does, it certainly cannot be linked to a specific strategy or campaign.

**This is not the time to axe your marketing budget, but to be smarter about it.**

Sometimes, leadership comes to the realization that their marketing is out of date. What worked well in the past is not working now, and they understand that the speed and virility with which information moves and has impact on the market is something they need to harness. However, knowing what to do now is the problem.

While marketing may not be every CEO's cup of tea, there is no mystery about what to do, and success can be pinned to specific tactics. It is incumbent upon business leadership to at least know the basics of smart marketing, and then obtain the services of a marketing professional who has a proven track record of improved sales.

## The Basics

Some fundamental realities have had a huge impact on marketing this last number of years. First and foremost is the availability of any kind of information someone could want. Exponential development of digital technology has created overwhelming amounts of data out there. The vast availability - rather, the bombarding presence - of advertising means that marketers are competing for attention in a noisy world. That barrage of information further paralyzes and weakens consumers' attention spans.

Print mailers, newspapers, radio, and even TV advertising have fallen out of vogue because of the availability and proliferation of digital marketing. Now marketing gurus talk about search engine optimization marketing, banners, pop-ups, and videos that adorn websites and social media ads. And all of this is much more easily executed and much more cost effective than traditional marketing media.

Digital technology is an incredible tool in the hands of marketers, but it has also given tremendous control to consumers. Internet users, whether willingly or unwittingly, influence what they see simply by choosing what they view and engage. Therefore, while cheap and easy, today's marketing efforts must be extremely time sensitive, responsive, and targeted. The marketer's job is to command attention and then keep it and nurture it, which is not always as easy as it may sound.

## Understand Your Ideal Buyer

As the company director, you can most likely identify your target market: businesses with printing needs, local roofing contractors, health conscious individuals looking for information and a good gym to join, imported automobile owners - the typical, every-day kinds of organizations and individuals who need services, goods, or information in order to accomplish what they want to do. However, are you able to narrow down your ideal buyer even more? For example, you may say that most of your customers are roofing contractors. But are they mostly new-build residential contractors? If they are mostly new-build residential, do you do more business with second-generation family-owned builders or multi-million dollar contractors who are putting in whole subdivisions at a time?

Dive deeper into your target demographic. Of course, you do business with all of them, but it pays to know all you can about the one or two who 1) bring you the most revenue, 2) need what you best provide.

About your roofing contractors: Do they build all over the continent, or mainly in one type of weather pattern? Are those who request the bids the decision-makers or just detail-gatherers? What kind of purchasing process do they have to go through? Are your buyers spending time on builds themselves, or do they take all their feedback from project managers and contractor foremen? The answers to these kinds of questions begin to sharpen the focus on exactly who you best serve. Knowing this will give you knowledge and ideas as to where to find them.

Basic understandings should be augmented by diligent searches for clues as to who your target is. There are rich demographic databases available to search, and you should also be directly questioning and surveying your customers and clients. You may or may not be involved in this - your marketing executive should be directing this hunt. But this kind of knowledge should drive your marketing - not guesswork.

## Find Your Ideal Buyer

You must know your target audience in order to know exactly what they want, need, and where they can be found. Are they on Facebook looking for recommendations of services? Are they online using specific keywords? Deeper understanding of target audience behaviour and demographics is key to reaching them effectively.

Knowing your target audience will also inform the tactics you use to reach them most effectively. Social media blasts around certain holidays or seasonal shifts? Regular email newsletters to nurture leads over time? Cause and affiliate marketing to attract cause-conscious proponents and their colleagues? Direct mail to curated mailing lists?

While most marketing is electronically based, there are still potential customers who look in the telephone directory or their mailbox for pertinent information sources. Again, know your ideal buyer.

# Common Marketing Mistakes

Following are the most common marketing mistakes, some of which can be corrected quickly. You may see an immediate uptick of sales.

## Not Having a Website

This is a huge mistake. Research indicates that nearly half of small businesses do not have a website because they think that since they serve locally, they do not need one. However, 90% or more of consumers research online before they go to businesses to purchase, even in their own communities. This alone should convince you to create a website.[3]

While it is possible to build your own website for free or next to nothing, this is inadvisable. You do not have to put thousands of dollars toward this. Find a professional website builder who can knowledgeably steer you through the critical site elements and help you determine your most advantageous presentation. A website can and should be updated regularly, so get something basic up, and refine it in the near future.

## Not Tracking Results

This is inexcusable these days, particularly with the metrics readily available on your digital platforms. 'If you can't measure it, you can't improve it', said Peter Drucker, and if you do not evaluate the Return on Investment (ROI) of your marketing efforts, you have no idea what is working and what is not - no idea what to change and what to keep doing. You know this is no way to do Research & Development, but it is also no way to do marketing. The only way you know you are doing something wrong is the fact that your customers are not finding you.

## Not Marketing at All

If you do not have some kind of presence on the web, no one will find you. You might think of pulling the marketing dollars out of the operating budget, and you may find reasons not to spend on marketing, but the loss of purchasing clients will far outpace the number of those who discover you accidentally. You do not have to have a huge budget and monthly campaigns. At the very least, create an attractive and useful website with evergreen content and proper Search Engine Optimization (SEO) to keep your site toward the top of the search results. Focus on a few small social media outlets, track your results, and develop what works.

## Incorrect Use of Social Media

When evaluating your ideal customer or client, you should be able to confidently conclude which social media platforms your ideal customer frequents. Then you can design your marketing messages. Social media marketing for the sake of social media marketing - because the gurus said you should - is simply throwing your money away.

Understand how each platform works and how to take best advantage of it. Additionally, the trends on and between the social media platforms, and who uses them, shift quickly and often. Your marketing professional should be able to stay abreast of these fluctuations and keep your marketing messages consistent on the outlets that you find are successful.

## Brand Inconsistency

Your brand is your appearance and your message: colour, logo, font, tag line, placement, and so on. Inconsistency over time will confuse your target buyers or convince them to go elsewhere. It is likely that at some point down the line, you will need to overhaul your brand and update the look and feel of your whole presence.

## Separating Marketing and Sales

Commonly, these two groups work separately from each other, but should plan and execute in close cooperation with each other. Marketing needs to be able to help the sales team with the 'heavy lifting': good sales materials, outreach support, and nurture potential customers toward the purchase. Sales needs to communicate back to marketing about what works and what does not. Sales may also be able to report observations about target buyers and indicate trends that should be taken into account.

## Lack of Positioning

Marketing just to increase sales will work for a while, but the work that will create a wider and sturdier customer base over the long run follows your position in the market. Market toward your ideal client, focusing on what you can do to meet their needs. Every message should flow straight to the ideal buyer from your Unique Selling Proposition (USP).

You may have discovered, when delving deeply into your ideal buyer, that you have been targeting one type of customer all along, when your best product or service should actually be offered to an entirely different audience. Then you may have to choose whether you will redirect your best marketing efforts, or perhaps change your best service or product offering to better capture the people who are available and willing to buy.

## Selling on the Wrong Platform

Businesses who sell on such platforms as Amazon or Shopify may find that they are missing a large portion or all of a target demographic by not being present on different platforms. It should be an easy matter to set up shop on new platforms - inexpensive in comparison to potential sales. Do not disdain the smaller, less known platforms for lack of breadth of reach. Buyers tend to be loyal to one or two shopping sites, and while you may have exactly what they need, if you are not where they shop, they will shop from your competitors.

───

It is not necessary to have an in-house marketing department. There are many marketing experts who can capture your brand and message quickly and help you create a consistent and effective marketing program, even part time. Get referrals locally or look online at any of many online communities or professional job boards. Regardless of where you find someone, take the time to verify references and measurable success stories before you hire. A savvy marketing guru is a wise investment that you cannot afford to ignore.

Monitor the return on your current marketing investments. Understand what is working and do not change it. Understand what is not working and stop it.

**"**

**If you can't
measure it,
you can't
improve it.**

*~Peter Drucker*

## CHAPTER 8

# Solution #5: Capitalize on Tax Provisions

**Chapter Summary** *Taxes figure heavily in the financial landscape of every company, both those taxes that deplete the bottom line and those that can be used to boost the bottom line. Highly qualified local tax attorneys (not just the CPA) should be consulted regarding every available advantage in both commonly known tax reliefs, as well as the more obscure provisions available in local jurisdictions.*

----

The HM Revenue & Customs, Internal Revenue Service, Canada Revenue Agency, *ad nauseum* - one of these agencies is likely part of the reason you are undertaking extreme measures to keep the company afloat. It is tempting to miss or delay a payment or two of the employer-submitted portions of national and local income taxes and other mandatory payroll deductions. However, the collecting agencies will exercise powerful sanctions to enforce compliance if you get behind, as you likely know all too well.

The taxman may also be part of your solution. There may be viable, tax-related strategies of which your company accountant or CPA is not aware. These tactics can lower the demands on your operating budget in terms of income, employment, sales, and excise taxes. While there are compelling reasons to pay what is owed on time, there is no need to pay more than is legitimately owed.

Following is an incomplete list of tax saving tactics intended to give you an idea of the types and depth of tax savings you may be able to implement. Some corporate tax savings tactics, or some variation thereof, are typical around the globe, while others are applicable only within local regions. The point is that while you know of the big ones, you may be eligible for other tax savings that can be strategized to make a difference.

You should consult with a well-qualified, local tax attorney who can evaluate your situation and identify ways to reduce your tax liability. If you have more than one physical site of business, consult for beneficial tax provisions in each locale.

## Generally Available Tax Reliefs

### Business Expenses

Any tax professional worth his salt should be able to provide you with a thorough list of everything you can claim as business expenses, as well as applicable limitations and exclusions. Review as to whether you and your staff are properly recording and submitting all allowable expenses. You may be surprised at how much these paltry amounts add up to over the course of a year.

The current Annual Investment Allowance in the United Kingdom is £1MM[4] as of this writing, although this is scheduled to reduce in January 2020. This amount can be used to write off expenses toward running your business, like new equipment or new computers. Amounts claimed will offset against your tax bill annually, prorated.

Check for permissible variations in calculations. In the United States, companies who claim expenses of using a personal vehicle for business can claim actual costs, or they can use the IRS standard mileage rate. With accurate records, one over the other may provide a good savings.

In the vein of expense deductions, check the best ways to claim depreciation. Canadian businesses deduct the purchase costs of their depreciable property over a period of time, but they are not required to claim the cost in the year it was realized. The Capital Cost Allowance can be used as much or as little as desired any given year. Look ahead for the best strategy toward offsetting a larger income tax bill.

Some locations allow capital gains reporting and payments to be prorated over time. Be sure to calculate your advantages in terms of other expenses now or later. For example, find out whether any current losses can be offset by reporting and paying on the full gain in the year of the sale.

## Retirement Plan Contributions

In the United States, family and individual-owned companies might be in a position to take advantage of arrangements that provide increased tax-advantaged retirement contributions and reduced tax liability. The result would be more cash to plow back into the company.

Other nations will have their own version of retirement and pension plans. Check to see how directing contributions will affect your portions of employment or income taxes. Be sure to consult a qualified independent retirement planner who works with a tax attorney specializing in retirement and pension contingencies.

## Deferred Income and Accelerated Deductions

At the end of the tax year, some receivables can be delayed and reported in the following year, to avoid declaring the income in the current year, perhaps by sending invoices out a few days later than normal. Similarly, paying bills in the current year rather than after the turn of the tax year may allow you to take the deduction for the current year.

## Charitable Donations

In Canada, donations to registered charitable organizations over the amount of $200.00 result in an increased tax credit because they are assessed at a higher rate. Charitable donations are typically used to reduce tax burden, but every country has its own rules. While charitable donations are not likely if you are in the red, assess whether any were indeed paid out and take full advantage of available credits.

## Domestic versus Foreign Production and Income

Manufacturers can take advantage of a variety of breaks granted to businesses who keep processes in the country, or who ship overseas. Foreign title passage allows for differentiation of domestic or foreign sourced income, thus potentially reducing tax burden assessed on income. Another permissible way to reduce potential tax bills is to hold rather than repatriate income from overseas business locations.

### Payroll Tax Savings

Hiring and maintaining an employee means a considerable outlay in PAYE and NIC taxes on a consistent basis. However, under current regulation, corporate income taxes can be reduced by up to 30% when hiring. Reduced corporate tax pay-out can translate into increased after-tax profits and increased shareholder value. Hiring decisions during these cash-flow-increase efforts should be carefully evaluated.

### Creative Industry Tax Relief

If your business is related to the creation and making of certain films, games, theatre, and audio-visual productions, you may qualify for tax relief.

### Research and Development Tax Relief

Businesses involved in scientific and technological advances may be eligible for tax relief on their profits. Small to medium enterprises qualify for a different level of relief. Demonstrable success in your project will qualify you for further relief percentages.

### 'Patent Box'

If your profits are exclusively from patented inventions, you own and license particular patents, and were involved in the development of these patents, your company may benefit from a 10% tax rate.

### 'Credit Interest'

When your company is in the black and you can manage with directing a bit less cash back into the business, take a look at the option of paying your HMRC portions early and getting interest back from the government. This takes some prognostication and planning, but it may be a legitimate savings in the future.

## In the USA

### 'Accountable Plans'

Accountable plans arrangements allow employers to reimburse employees for business expenses without having to treat the reimbursed money as income. In these cases, the company pays less FICA and unemployment tax, and the employee pays less income tax.

### Penalties for Late and Non-Performance

Penalties or fines paid for late performance or non-performance of contracts are frequently deductible. If you have had to pay such fines in the course of your troubles, check if they qualify to be deducted.

### Tax Deductions and Credits for Employment of Disabled Individuals

A variety of tax credits and deductions are available for US employers who accommodate and hire individuals with disabilities. Some are one time credits and some may be repeated year by year.

## In Canada

### Income Splitting

The income splitting strategy allows small business owners to transfer - as wages or dividends - a portion of their earnings to a family member who falls into a lower income rate. Lower taxes are paid on the transferred amount, and the tax bill on the remaining income is also less than had it been taxed at the higher rate. By rule, the family member must be treated as a regular employee in terms of paperwork and requisite tasks commensurate with the pay. The dividend strategy requires a properly registered corporation, but the family members do not have to be employees.

### Quick Accounting Harmonized Sales Tax

Small business owners in Canada may be able to use quick accounting method tactics that permit charging the Harmonized Sales Tax to your customers but remitting only about half of it to the CRA. Also, certain tactics would allow business owners to keep cash in the company coffers that would otherwise be taxed as personal income, thus reducing personal tax and increasing corporate cash flow.

### Apprenticeship Tax Credit

If your company hires tradespeople, hiring an apprentice within the first two years of his or her program can be worth a $2,000 tax credit.

## Research and Development Tax Relief

The same tax relief for science and technology development available in the United Kingdom is available as a tax credit in Canada.

———

A thorough tax audit should look beyond the major categories of income and payroll taxes, into the myriad other taxes and claims around capital, losses, imports and excise, sales and VAT, charities, and others. While they may not be widely advertised as viable options, there may be any number of deductions, credits, deferrals, exemptions, abatements, and incentives you can legitimately use.

Do everything you can to both lower the total income you pay taxes on and reduce the total tax owed on that income. If you are not confident that your tax professional is doing everything possible to save you dollars and pounds, bring in an outside professional who is current with tax planning and business law to review your situation and recommend the most advantageous arrangements.

Have your tax advisor present you with every option available, including new codes that have passed but are not yet active in locations where you have a physical presence. Some measures are temporary, such as the tax breaks set in place in the wake of extremely damaging hurricanes such as Katrina (2005) or Harvey (2017). Charitable contributions were raised for both individuals and businesses, but this lasted only through the end of the year.

It is likely that taking advantage of any tax savings will not help you out quickly, except those involving payments that you make on a regular basis, like payroll taxes. Even so, if the fiscal year is just around the corner, a deep look at your liabilities can significantly lower your pending income tax bill.

Regardless of the bill you must pay next, part of your larger audit should be to ensure that your accounting software is set up to take the proper deductions on a rolling basis, and that your tax accountant is aware of every measure you are undertaking.

There is nothing to be lost and potentially much to be gained by consulting a knowledgeable and local tax professional for a critical evaluation of the company. Going forward, this should be done at set intervals, in order to stay abreast of legislation changes.

CHAPTER 9

# That Was Not Quite Enough

**Chapter Summary** *When bankruptcy seems inescapable, the business owner or director can choose liquidation and winding up either voluntarily or at the hands of creditors. The next option is Administration and exploration as to whether or not the company can be saved. Those first prospects typically leave creditors the least satisfied and produce the most ill will and expense, not to mention the potential investigation of a director and possible fraudulent or wrongful trading charges.*

———

Suppose you have a million dollars' worth of creditors hammering at your door, including the tax man, and you cannot even make payroll next week. By this time in your reading, you have a pretty good feeling that you are in trouble regardless of what you do. You wonder how cowardly it would be to quietly close up shop and board a boat to the nearest desert island.

It is very simple. Trading while insolvent is illegal. As the company director, if you cannot make payroll, you should not even have the doors open. The government takes a long view of trading while insolvent. Once you realize that you are insolvent, you must make a quick decision. If a statutory demand by a creditor is uncontested and unpaid for a set number of days

(21 in the UK), and the amount owed is over a certain amount, that creditor can petition and initiate the bankruptcy proceedings.

You have these choices at this point:

01. **Let the creditors file a Winding Up Petition against you and enter liquidation.**

02. **Volunteer to undergo liquidation via Voluntary Creditor Liquidation or Chapter 7.**

03. **Volunteer to go under Administration.**

04. **Undertake a Company Voluntary Arrangement or Chapter 11 Reorganization.**

## Liquidation and Winding Up

These first two options are obviously the least appealing, whether it is voluntary or creditor-instigated. Winding up means

— **the director's employment is lost, as well as all of the company's employees.**

— **if the director has put up any personal assets as collateral, they will be lost to the creditors.**

— **director's accounts must be paid.**

— **for at least one year during and following a winding up, directors may not be involved in the management or formation of another company.**

— **an investigation into the director's actions for the past three years will be opened, and any misconduct will result in sanctions.**

— **a bankruptcy record will remain on the director's credit file for a number of years, hampering ability to obtain credit during that period.**

— **customers will be forced to locate another resource.**

— **to recoup their losses, the vendors will have to fight to get a share of the assets.  These are ugly battles with poor resolutions.**

## Other Things to Know:
## Pros and Cons of Liquidation

*Liquidation is an option when directors find their companies in desperate financial straits. Compulsory or involuntary liquidation happens when creditors pursue repayment petitions for winding up - that is, closing the company and selling assets to recover their losses.*

*However, voluntary liquidation is also a viable option when the directors, owners, and other controlling stakeholders are convinced that debts will not be paid short of a miracle. Secured creditors first, then insolvency practitioners, then remaining creditors - each take their share of the proceeds of sale.*

*There are some benefits to voluntary liquidation.*

— Unpaid debt is written off. Unless personal guarantees were made, liquidating directors are not legally liable to pay sums owed by the business itself.

— Liquidating directors are free to get on with their lives, including starting a new business if desired.

— Legal action against the company is halted, and creditors may not begin new legal action, as long as the director did not put up personal assets as collateral.

— Liquidated employees can claim redundancy or unemployment, unpaid wages, vacation pay, and other payments. Some of the payments may be made from sale of assets, others from employment insurances already paid by the company.

— Leases and purchase agreements are cancelled, and back payments may be requested from the insolvency practitioners.

— Court proceedings can be avoided.

— Liquidation costs are less than those involved in the professional fees and court costs associated with Company Voluntary Arrangement, or Chapter 11.

*Looking at things this way makes voluntary liquidation fairly attractive in the face of financial constraints too steep to surmount. However, there are some negative outcomes.*

*A trained and licensed Insolvency Practitioner will be appointed by the Bankruptcy Court, the Insolvency Service, or by the directors/ stakeholders. This individual, depending on the situation, will advise the directors or take complete control of the company before it is shuttered. Unless winding up is initiated voluntarily, the company directors have no control over how assets are disposed of and how proceeds are disbursed.*

— As part of the liquidation process, the insolvency practitioner is required to open investigations into the conduct of the directors, owners, and other principle actors. Detailed reports will be submitted and if wrongful or fraudulent trading is determined, the results can be disastrous to individuals found guilty.

— If it is determined that liquidation was undertaken in order to sidestep repayment, company directors may end up personally liable for company debts.

— In any case, director's accounts will have to be repaid.

— All assets will be sold - nothing can be retained with which to start a new business. The insolvency professional and lawyers will collect their fees and all the creditors will be satisfied as much as possible.

— If any personal assets like homes, boats, real estate, and so on were put up as personal guarantee for company debts, those assets will be taken.

— While they can file for unemployment payments and look for new jobs, liquidation means loss of jobs, including the managers' jobs. There is no guarantee that these knowledgeable persons will be available to help get a new business off the ground.

— Credit or financing for future endeavours may be impaired.

— In the United States, debt forgiveness may be taxable.

# Administration

The next choice is to seek Administration. When Administration is chosen voluntarily, rather than mandated by courts in response to a winding up petition, the directors and shareholders, or others with voting interest, appoint a professionally trained and licensed insolvency practitioner (IP). This individual will have control; directors have no say. The IP will investigate, and then decide whether the company should be

- **closed down altogether.**
- **sold and the proceeds distributed to those with claims.**
- **put into a CVA in attempt to keep it open.**

As mentioned, the option of closing down altogether is clearly the least desirable.

# Sale under Administration

The outcome of a company sale at this point tends to net low satisfaction. The Administration process can take up to a year, during which time Administrators may be leery about continuing business as usual. Compounding this, in the United Kingdom, for the duration of the Administration, all invoices, purchase orders, sales flyers, websites, and so on, must state that the company is under Administration, which tends to erode public confidence. It may become difficult to maintain the good will of the customer or client base. Vendors are loathe to extend current contracts to the purchasers as they are sure to lose everything owed by the original owners. Individuals of the staff may or may not be transferred over to the new company and maintain their jobs. Some of the time, the directors are able to inform and influence decisions, but the Administrator may also choose to remove the directors altogether and appoint new directors. Considerable rebuilding must be done in the event of a sale.

There are instances of a Pre-pack Administration in which a sale agreement is made prior to the formal Insolvency Practitioner's appointment. The goal is to create a new company that can go on with minimal loss of trade. However, this will be subject to scrutiny, as such a tactic is often used by unscrupulous directors to offload debt and continue running a company with no repercussions.

During an Administration, the Administrator is required to investigate the directors' activities for the three years leading up to the Administration. Stiff sanctions may adversely impact future plans.

The likelihood of saving the business and returning monies to the creditors falls drastically when the Administrator can effectively shut out or remove the managers and directors. However, there are two methods which allow maintenance of personal control, the greatest chance of survival, and satisfied creditors:

**01.** The Limited Liability Partnership (LLP)

**02.** Company Voluntary Arrangement (CVA)

In these next two chapters, I will present an overview of the Limited Liability Partnership (LLP) and the Company Voluntary Arrangement (CVA) as they occur in the UK, followed with comparisons as they are structured in the USA. Those in other jurisdictions should look into the options available to them. By and large, they will consist of some variations of what is described below.

Does liquidation look inevitable? Restructuring your entire business and reorganizing your debts are the tools used to stop the haemorrhaging and restore viable life to the enterprise. These options require profound determination to keep the business intact, even while feeling as though you have finally lost complete control.

## Other Things to Know:
## Director Investigation

*The Insolvency Service or the Bankruptcy Trustee will conduct investigations in three cases: formal insolvency proceedings of administrative receivership; voluntary and involuntary liquidation; and when misconduct is suspected as Administrations proceed. Anyone who was in active control for a period of time leading up to the declaration of insolvency will come under scrutiny, whether company directors, acting directors, or those who have instructed directors - legally appointed or not. Accounting and other company records will be reviewed, and further interviews will pursue specific instances of conduct. Creditors and suppliers, stakeholders, employees, accountants, lawyers, lenders, tax preparers and other advising professionals may be questioned. This is a civil inquiry, although if criminal activity is suspected, the police and other pertinent agencies will be brought in.*

*Allegations of unfit conduct may be raised upon discovery of the following situations:*

- Failure to keep creditor interests above business interests
- Failure to properly submit required filings
- Failure to pay tax and employment taxes
- Purposeful reduction of amounts available to repay creditors
- Failure to follow regulatory guidelines
- Lack of cooperation with investigation professionals

*Sufficient evidence of fraudulent trading will result in the director's disqualification from being a director, or being part of forming or running any company for up to 15 years. Conviction may also require the director to pay fines and fees or be made personally liable to pay compensation to creditors who have suffered material loss. Last but not least is the lingering shadow of stigma attached to investigation and disqualification.*

## Other Things to Know:
## Wrongful or Fraudulent Trading

*If you are concerned that your company is insolvent, your primary priority is to act in the best interests of your creditors, not necessarily to guide the business out of trouble. Failure to look closer and act accordingly can have harsh repercussions on the business and upon your personal life, your reputation, and your future. Once creditors have petitioned against you and you are looking at liquidation, whether voluntary or otherwise, an insolvency practitioner is required to investigate and report on the directors' activity for a given period of time leading up to the insolvency.*

*In **wrongful trading**, directors are acting irresponsibly, by not taking every step available to minimize creditor loss or avoid insolvency. Examples of such behaviour would include failure to file returns or pay employment taxes correctly and on time, showing preference to certain creditors over others, or taking a salary that cannot be justified by the actual revenue. Such actions are a civil offence, and directors can be held personally liable for the company's debts. They may also be disqualified, fined, or sent to jail.*

*In **fraudulent trading**, which is a criminal offence, the directors intentionally act for their own benefit, defrauding creditors on what is owed. Fraudulent actions may include accepting credit knowing that the payments will not be made, or taking customer orders knowing that the orders will not be fulfilled, or selling assets below fair market value before liquidation. The penalties for fraudulent trading are more severe than those for wrongful trading, and include longer disqualification or prison time, in addition to being responsible for a greater portion of the company debts.*

# CHAPTER 10

# Restructuring the Company

**Chapter Summary** *The Limited Liability Partnership is a major structural change that can be used not only to keep a company viable but also to increase productivity. In this option, every employee is made a partner, which has the immediate effect of ending payments for PAYE, FICA, and income taxes. This cash is kept in the coffers as working capital. Employees-turned-partners handle their own taxes and enjoy ownership in the business.*

———

Law has long dealt with limits to the personal liability of individuals involved in business against debt and loss incurred by that business. However, the effectiveness of these laws continues to be circumvented by other legally sanctioned mechanisms, like requirement for personal guarantees, floating charges, and debt enforcement agencies. Those building businesses these days are under considerable pressure to consider minute details in their legal structure so they can offer their resources to the community without fear of succumbing to complete loss in the eventuality of adverse events.

A carefully constructed Limited Liability Partnership proves to be quite adept at securing assets and protecting various concerns from creditor action. In the situation of a distressed company, changing the legal structure to an LLP will create some boundaries against aggressive creditors, and just as importantly, create the added benefit of putting a worthwhile percentage of a business's annual revenue back into the cash flow.

To over simplify it, every employee is made a partner, much like the partners in a law firm, where everyone is acting as a business owner responsible for their contribution to the profits of the enterprise and with entitlement to participate in those profits. For a distressed business, about six weeks are all that is needed to build up between 10% and 15% of the annual revenue. Income is no longer draining away in the form of employment and income taxes, but is available toward working capital.

To be sure, there is much more to an LLP than simply 'making everybody a partner'. As I said, careful thought must be put into a number of things, such as:

— **Management structure for clear decision-making, ensuing obligations, and authorizations.**
— **Ensuring that if one entity goes under, the others can carry on.**
— **Protection of intangible assets like software, trademarks, patents, customer lists, brand, proprietary data, or methodologies; and of physical assets like equipment, inventory, and real estate.**
— **Protection of shareholder interests.**
— **Ensuring that the resulting structure is legally contracted and robust enough that it cannot be easily undermined.**
— **Minimising requirements for personal guarantees.**

Separate legal entities may be formed to handle different business roles and function alongside the LLP. For example, a Limited Company (LTD) would hold the intangible and tangible assets and serve as a treasury and billing department. Another LTD may act as the vehicle handling investment funds, interest, shares and dividends. LLP or LTD trading entities may be created to trade under the licenses provided by the LTD holding those intangible assets, engage the customers in sales and service, undertake in commercial contracts with suppliers, and distribute profits to partners. By these efforts, actual or contingent liabilities are separated from assets which are otherwise vulnerable to exploitation by creditors and their methods of recovery.

All existing contracts and agreements with customers, vendors, stakeholders, lenders, and investors will come under scrutiny as they are updated to reflect new leadership, new names, and new relationships.

This will be a chance to double check against potential gaps or loopholes through which creditors or other leakage may do damage.

## New Partner Status

As partners, all recent former employees will now have claim to a stake of the profits. Instead of a salary received as a cost to the business, they receive advance portions of those stakes. Partner responsibility and compensation packages will be defined in the legal documents. There are no hard and fast rules as to what partner-ownership looks like in terms of percentage of ownership, apportionment of profit and loss, channels of decision making, and dispute resolution.

The directors are able to make this change without employee buy-in, but generally speaking, company-wide morale is boosted by this move. Fiscal responsibility for company success tends to bring out more interest and engagement on an individual level, rather than the make-work mindset of those punching the clock for a regular paycheck. Everyone in the company, from top to bottom, is a business owner and invited to act accordingly. Decisions are made with the benefit of discussion and understanding of implications on every level, rather than by fiat from the executive suite. Everyone partakes in business successes proportionate to their stake.

Liability protections are built into the legal structure, so that while they may experience shorter draws during a hard time, partner members are not personally liable for company insolvency.

New partner status necessitates acting as self-employed, and thereby filing self-employment taxes. If this is mysterious to individuals, provisions can be made to withhold tax and assist with the filings, either in-house alongside the human resources staff, or externally.

Also, LLP members are responsible for their own medical, disability, and income insurances. The rise in the last decade of the 'freelancer economy' has seen a corresponding rise in traditional insurance concepts and hybrid co-ops that cater specifically to the self-employed. Offerings for the whole group of newly-minted self-employed can be negotiated and presented as part of the partnership compensation.

In the UK, laws are evolving to extend statutory rights of employees to the new LLP members created by the structure change. For example, the statutory protections afforded to 'workers' under the Employment Rights

Act 1996 already apply to LLP members. However, as with the insurance provisions, the statutory rights and others granted will be negotiated and agreed upon in the creation of the LLP.

There are some differences in details between the United States, Canada and the United Kingdom, but the concept is generally the same, in that restructuring puts a greater portion of revenue back into the company's cash flow rather than those monies being payable in insurance and income taxes. Partners have specified protections from the actions of other partners and are not destined to go down with the whole ship.

While the UK model is applicable across the United Kingdom, each state in the United States governs the formation and operation of Limited Liability Partnerships. The LLP is an option for any type of business, not just architects, lawyers, physicians, accountants, and similar high-liability-risk occupations. In Canada, the various provinces permit LLPs for just those occupations, or for all businesses.

———

Undertaking a legal restructuring from limited company to LLP is not an easy overnight solution, but it should be seriously considered. An adequately and properly executed LLP (and accompanying organizations) would require several months' to a year's labour, plus the cost of knowledgeable and skilled legal professionals. Those costs would have to come out of revenue or new financing, which at the offset might prove difficult to obtain. Still, the option should not be dismissed off-hand by the company director who is convinced that the business can be turned around and run at profit, and who has the intestinal fortitude to begin the formidable task.

# Reorganizing the Debt

**Chapter Summary** *While there are significant differences between the UK's Company Voluntary Arrangement and the US's Chapter 11, the essentials remain the same. Creditor recovery actions are halted and debts are renegotiated. Debt reorganization efforts can end in much lower monthly debt payments over time, yet yield much higher monetary recovery by the creditors. With a lower regular repayment burden, cash flow can be used to keep the business open and operating legally. In the United States, the process may be undertaken according to federal or state statues, or entirely outside of the courts, in an out-of-court workout.*

———

Where there are a few rays of hope and a lot of determination to keep the company open, distressed directors can initiate one last 'big hammer' as the finishing effort: debt reorganization. Company Voluntary Arrangements (CVA) and Chapter 11s happen all the time with big name companies, such as Allied Healthcare, House of Fraser, Toys R Us, and Sears Holding. They are also viable options for mid- and small-sized enterprises, even if less common. On the whole, the outcomes are much more attractive than the first three options of voluntary or involuntary winding up or voluntary administration.

# In the UK - Company Voluntary Arrangement

The action of beginning the Company Voluntary Arrangement proceedings brings immediate relief in several ways.

First, it brings a shield down around the company against creditors and their proceedings. By law, once a CVA is initiated, you are not required to pay creditors. At the very least, this means that money is not now streaming away. If the phone rings and a creditor is on the line, all that needs to be said is that you are commencing a CVA and that you are not required to pay.

This protection lasts roughly four to eight weeks. During this time, the business can still run. If you can still generate and fulfil sales, you will have revenue with which to keep operating. Technically, you do not have to pay rent or employees, but the best wisdom would tell you to pay those employees, because they are what is keeping the revenue coming in. You do not want to pinch so hard that you force your best assets away.

With the wolves called off, your CVA professional will now contact each of your creditors one at a time, and offer a deal. He will propose a settlement of something between 20 and 40 cents to the dollar for what is owed. In my experience with hundreds of CVAs, some 90 percent of the time, the creditors will agree to such an agreement. The reason they agree to such a loss is that if the company goes out of business, they will not get anything at all of what is owed them. With the company remaining open and trading, they will recoup at least a portion of their money.

A certain majority of the creditors and the stakeholders has to agree to the terms, so there will be some back and forth finessing by a skilled CVA practitioner regarding the exact details to which everyone puts their signature. This will take six weeks or so.

Now, a million in debt is reduced to $200,000 to $400,000, just like that. In addition to reducing the debt, the legal agreement worked out with the creditors also spells out the repayment schedule. Typically, the repayment of that reduced debt is amortized over two to five years. That million dollars of debt is suddenly now much more manageable.

During the time the CVA arrangements were being worked out, the company has continued with business while not having to pay debts. Everything that has come in has accrued in the bank, so now there is even a bit of surplus cash in the bank. In just a few weeks, the company is once again solvent and legally trading. Once the terms of the Company Voluntary Arrangement are all set and signed, the shield around the company is removed. Trading goes on and debt payments are made at more manageable terms.

Costs of CVA professional services will be paid from the current revenue, however the expenses for a turnaround will be far less than fees charged by liquidating insolvency practitioners.

## Advantages to CVA over Administration

— Even if made on the strong advice of a business rescue practitioner, the company directors make their own decisions.

— It takes 4 - 8 weeks to work out details and execute agreements versus potentially a year to conclude Administration.

— Focus shifts from putting out fires and trying to placate creditors to operating the business and creating a viable plan.

— Jobs are maintained, including the directors' positions.

— The business remains open and trading, so there is no loss of customer or vendor base and no need to rebuild good will from scratch.

## A Brief History of insolvency in the UK vs. US

As described in an article by Andrew Jackson and Scott Taylor in The Gazette Official Public Record,[5] the United States and the United Kingdom have the same general structures in place for dealing with insolvency, but it is helpful to recognize a few historical cultural differences between the two nations to understand the bankruptcy-related differences between the two jurisdictions.

The United States has been borrower-friendly, with high risk traditionally rewarded and failure pardoned. The mammoth risks undertaken by individuals first settling the West and those investing in the industrial revolution have traditionally brought rewards of great achievement and success. Failure is not so much fatal as the opportunity to try again. This has meant, in terms of financial risk undertaken by those lending to motivated borrowers, that the risk must be carefully considered. Thus, in some states, it is nearly impossible to enforce a debt judgment.

Across the pond, the United Kingdom has been more lender-friendly. This stems from centuries of feudal life, in which unpaid taxes to the lord or monarch reduced most to a kind of slavery. Growth of international markets in the Middle Ages solidified the practice of swift seizure of assets upon failure to pay debt. Resulting laws have guarded risk more closely by demanding responsibility. Recent efforts in the UK reflect a trend toward rescue and rehabilitation rather than liquidation or administrative receivership.[6]

In the UK, a bankruptcy filing is voluntary by the debtor or involuntary by the creditors. In the States, the majority of filings are voluntary and bankruptcy is seen as a relief. The rare involuntary bankruptcy filings in the US are usually initiated by creditors trying to enforce their own rights.

## In the US - Chapter 11 Plan of Reorganization

Chapter 11 Plan of Reorganization is the formal legal United States equivalent of the Company Voluntary Arrangement, in that it addresses the same issue in roughly the same manner, with similar outcomes. After the initial formal filing to the United States Bankruptcy Court, the debtor becomes 'debtor in possession', and is granted the rights and duties of handling the proceedings, excepting any required investigations. At this point, the automatic stay is extended, under which creditors may not initiate, enforce, or appeal judgments against the debtor, neither for claims already made nor for new claims after the declaration of bankruptcy. A secured creditor, however, may take certain actions to stake actionable claim on pertinent collateral or improve their positions pending settlement.

The business will continue to run as usual, with some constraints, and under supervision of the court. A trustee may or may not be assigned by the US Bankruptcy Court, depending on the size of the filing entity and any suspected fraud, wrongdoing, or risk.

The debtor in possession has four months (120 days) during the automatic stay to submit a plan of reorganization.

The plan may consist of any or all parts of the following situations:

— **Renegotiation of total owed and the terms of repayment.**
— **Selling some of the assets and proceeds distributed to creditors.**
— **An investor provides a source of capital.**
— **Some portion of the remuneration is pursued by litigation over specified actions on the part of the company.**

After the 120 days, other interested parties, usually creditors, can file their own plans. If a Trustee is appointed by the Bankruptcy Court, this individual must create his own plan or recommend that the Chapter 11 proceedings be changed to a Chapter 7 bankruptcy liquidation. (It is possible to execute a liquidation under Chapter 11 which permits liquidation of assets in far more favourable terms than possible under Chapter 7.)

In the event of multiple plans filed, the court will determine which plan(s) meet requirements for confirmation. Amendments can be filed in response and/or objections filed. The court will examine the selected plan to ensure required provisions are met. Upon confirmation, the debtor will be discharged to operate the business under terms in the reorganization plan.

Reorganization in the United States can take a few months to a few years.

## Creditors Committee

The creditors committee, comprised of secured creditors, is responsible for determining whether or not the filing business should be liquidated instead of reorganized. If reorganization is approved, the committee is charged to negotiate the plan of reorganization between creditors and the debtor. This plan will specify repayment terms and schedules and any other reorganization that will take place, such as change of ownership, business structure, or management. An LLP reorganization may be part of the reorganization plan. The committee is also responsible to ensure that unsecured and other underrepresented creditors are treated as equitably as the secured creditors whose claims have priority.

## Pre-Packs

In the UK, a pre-pack is more of an Administration consideration than the CVA. In the US, a pre-packaged plan may be agreed upon prior to formal filing. A pre-package is simply an agreement in which general terms of reorganization are negotiated and confirmed with creditors before filing for Chapter 11. In a 'lock-up agreement' the creditors' votes of approval can be obtained in support of any plan to be drafted as long as it contains specified provisions. A 'pre-negotiated' Chapter 11 is used to negotiate with the higher priority creditors according to pre-understood expectations, but the final details are not hammered out until the Chapter 11 court has approved the basic provisions. Each of these cases has the advantage of shortening the time and money spent in court, therefore reducing the overall time that the entire process takes.

## Cost of Reorganization

Understandably, the longer it takes, and the more court dates that are required, the more costly the Chapter 11 proceeding will be. Fees are paid to the US Trustee for oversight, to lawyers, and to other advisors appointed by the creditor's committee. The expense of convincing the court that the plan of reorganization is viable can be the largest consideration when looking at a Chapter 11 solution.

All of that said, bankruptcy proceedings for very large companies involving $50M USD are handled at the federal bankruptcy level. More and more smaller companies are dealing with Chapter 11-type provisions at the state level, where progress tends to be quicker, less costly, and less visible to public scrutiny.

## Out-of-Court Workout

Empirical studies vary in their approaches and conclusions, but many find the success rate for Chapter 11 filings to be between ten and 27%.[7,8]

There are provisions in United States law to undertake reorganization of debt outside of bankruptcy court.

An Out-of-Court Workout can be used to successfully avoid formal Chapter 11 or Chapter 7 (liquidation) filing, the associated costs, and the inevitable expenditure of energy. The funds otherwise used to pay bankruptcy professionals and court costs can be paid to creditors. There are a few significant drawbacks to these efforts. One intractable creditor can render a workout useless and drive the company to court anyway. Bringing all the creditors together may create the occasion of an agreement to go ahead and force the debtor into bankruptcy, and may compel the sharing of information that is otherwise protected. There is no stay against creditors trying to enforce their rights while the plan is being worked out, so debt payments must continue and there is no surge of cash flow from those weeks of protection.

———

While labour intensive, CVAs, Chapter 11 Reorganizations, and their equivalents, are viable options for saving companies with a genuine shred of hope remaining. A debt reorganization, combined with a legal structure change to Limited Liability Partnership, is even more powerful.

## CHAPTER 12

# Who Should We Hire?

**Chapter Summary** *The success of your turnaround endeavours hinges heavily upon the professionals you select to work with. Seek a highly experienced insolvency practitioner and a turnaround consultant who comes with a verifiable track record of successful outcomes. Do not be persuaded by an insolvency lawyer who specializes in anything but company rescue.*

———

Now you are facing a daunting decision, one that has many implications for serious impact on many lives. There is a great deal of pressure on you, as the company director, to make the right decisions, at a time when you are likely questioning everything you have done up to now.

This is not the time to assume that those who have given you prior financial advice can provide the sound advice you need now.

Keep this in mind: Trained professionals tend to think and do what they are trained to do, and particularly to do what they have done repeatedly. This is not a good thing or a bad thing, but it should be recognized as a powerful influence on outcomes.

Consider the following scenario.

The Barrons, both age 72, owned and operated a very profitable business for many years, a solid service to the community. Eight years ago, they took a fair sum of money out of the business to invest. However, the investment failed. They took out a high interest loan to put the money back into the company, with personal guarantees of their house and two prized racehorses.

While the business was profitable, it was not lucrative enough to meet the demands of the high-interest debt. Soon, they could not make the tax payments, their vendors went unpaid, and then the letters came from the HMRC, threatening to close them down, just at retirement age.

Upon the suggestion of a business acquaintance, the Barrons consulted a well-recommended corporate turnaround specialist, who took a deep look at the situation. He offered to take over 51% of the company, restructure the debts, secure the house and horses, and keep the company open. The Barrons would maintain 49% of the company, enjoy a reasonable income, and be able to go to the races all week - the retirement they had envisioned. This sounded wonderful to the Barrons.

The Barrons mentioned this encounter to their trusted, long-time accountant, who advised them to talk to a bankruptcy lawyer. This they did, and the bankruptcy lawyer persuaded them that he could do the same thing without taking 51% of the company: restructure the debts, keep the house and horses, and keep the business running.

The Barrons went with the bankruptcy attorney. This individual restructured the debts, got 20 - 40 cents on the dollar for the creditors, and kept the house and the horses. However, after the bankruptcy attorney had taken his fees from the company cash flow, there was nothing left. The business closed anyway. The Barrons had to sell the house and the horses and settled into a meagre retirement.

When you are choosing a professional to handle a turnaround, you owe it to yourself to choose one who will work with your best interests at heart, and this means looking past impressive certifications and advertising to what they actually do all day long. Do the businesses they work on keep running, or do they fold after the fees are paid out? Do the business owners and managers really succeed in the end?

While they have served you well in what they understand intimately, your accountant or barrister simply may not have the best advice or the best contacts for you at this point. They will be advising you from their wisdom and set of references, which is right for the scope of what they do on a daily basis. Their wisdom is not worthless, but it is more likely that you need options outside those boxes right now.

In the same way, a bankruptcy professional will provide services and solutions within the scope of their training and practice. However, their intent is to do what they do, which is practice bankruptcy law and charge bankruptcy attorney fees. Their overriding mission is not a creative, win-win solution for all involved.

One way or another, you will have to retain the services of a bankruptcy attorney. But also consider the service of an insolvency turnaround consultant who is not necessarily a lawyer but who will do two things for you:

First, he or she will come up with a creative strategy to save the business. It might not look like anything you could have imagined, but at the end of the day, will be the best possible scenario for everyone. Your business stays open, your creditors get a portion of their money, and your professional does not take everything that is left for his fees.

Second, your turnaround consultant can take on most of the turnaround efforts burden, leaving you free to run and improve the business. If you end up working for the bankruptcy attorney to accomplish his ends, you are not getting ahead – you have only hired another problem.

Ask your current accounting or legal professionals if they can refer you to an experienced and successful turnaround consultant. Ask other colleagues or businesses who may be able to refer from their own experience.

Check online for bankruptcy professionals from the national certifying board in your country. They have lists of trained and certified or licensed individuals you can contact.

- — United States - American Board of Certification (abcworld.org)
- — United Kingdom - Association of Insolvency & Restructuring Advisors (aira.org)
- — Canada - Canadian Association of Insolvency and Restructuring Professionals (CAIRP.ca)
- — Global Association - Turnaround Management Association (turnaround.org)

Look at your prospective professional's website and determine if their specialty is liquidation, bankruptcy, or insolvency turnaround. It should be very clear. Then schedule a phone call and see which way their questions and suppositions seem to lean. Go ahead and take the trouble to get references from the businesses they have helped. Call or visit those former clients to find out exactly what the experience was like.

Have a personal interview with the professional you will be working with - not just the secretary or manager who hands out assignments. Be sure you feel comfortable, at the end of the conversation, with the way they talked about the things they emphasized, the promises they made, and the conditions they initially outlined.

If possible, select a professional who has experience in your industry.

Do not go with a well-recommended practitioner who will 'mainly do liquidations but I can help you save the business if that's what you want'. Go with an insolvency practitioner you are sure will get the best possible rate for your creditors, and put you in the best position going forward. Go with the practitioner who will strive to keep the company open and be a team member, not the one who will feel like an interloper just doing his job.

Finding yourself at the brink of insolvency does not automatically mean that you - or anyone - must lose. Turnaround depends on the efforts of individuals who are determined to explore every option and follow through with hard decisions by taking action.

"

The price of success is
hard work, dedication
to the job at hand, and
the determination that
whether we win or
lose, we have applied
the best of ourselves
to the task at hand.

*~Vince Lombardi*

# Conclusion

Paying your bills honourably is important to your sense of dignity and your reputation. So is doing the best you can by your employees.

Bringing your business back from the brink will not be easy. If it were easy, anyone could do it. Diagnosing where troubles lie and taking corrective actions require discernment and courage. Every element of the company is at stake - the company, livelihoods, reputations, services, and goods the community has relied upon. Going forward will require forging new relationships and possibly severing some existing alliances, both of which may be extremely uncomfortable for a period of time.

But imagine the alternative - closing down. Winding up is not inevitable. By implementing the options in this book, you may find the result of your turnaround is a stronger and more profitable company than you had ever thought possible.

# About Perry Anderson

Perry M. Anderson is a global investor and entrepreneur who has made over 30 investments in the past 18 years, through his private equity firm, Quadra Global Capital Corporation. He is sector agnostic and has considerable private equity experience across a diverse range of industries, including real estate, manufacturing, technology, media, restaurant/retail, construction, security, cyber-security, energy, and mining. In support of these investments, he has raised millions of dollars for early stage, growth, and pre-IPO companies.

Mr. Anderson is Canadian by nationality, has an MBA from Oxford University, and splits his time between homes in Vancouver and London.

# References

## Chapter 2

1.  Infographic. (August 2018). Frequently asked questions about
    small business. US Small Business Administration Office of
    Advocacy. Retrieved April 15, 2019 from https://www.sba.gov/
    sites/default/files/advocacy/Frequently-Asked-Questions-Small-
    Business-2018.pdf

## Chapter 5

2.  Key findings. (2018). Leadership: Driving innovation and
    delivering impact. The Deloitte Global Chief Procurement Officer
    Survey 2018. Deloitte and Odgers Berndtson. Retrieved April 15,
    2019 from https://www2.deloitte.com/content/dam/Deloitte/at/
    Documents/strategy-operations/deloitte-global-cpo-survey-2018.pdf

## Chapter 7

3.  Rampton, John. (September 24, 2015). The 10 most
    common small business marketing mistakes. Forbes.
    Retrieved April 15, 2019 from https://www.forbes.com/sites/
    johnrampton/2015/09/24/the-10-most-common-small-business-
    marketing-mistakes/#c2e4ec91f8c4

## Chapter 8

4.  Claim capital allowances. (2019) Gov.uk. Retrieved April 15, 2019
    from https://www.gov.uk/capital-allowances/annual-investment-
    allowance

## Chapter 11

5.   Jackson, A., & Taylor, S. (no date given) UK vs US debt recovery cultures and collections strategies. The Gazette.co.uk. Retrieved April 15, 2019 from https://www.thegazette.co.uk/insolvency/content/100263

6.   Report. (2007). Comparison of Chapter 11 of the United States Bankruptcy Code. Jonesday.com Retrieved April 15, 2019 from https://www.jonesday.com/files/Publication/1ec093d4-66fb-42a6-8115-be0694c59443/Presentation/PublicationAttachment/e5b46572-7aeb-4c34-ab2e-bee2f8f3d3c2/Comparison%20of%20Chapter%2011%20(A4).pdf

7.   Arnopol, M. M. (April 2014). Why have Chapter 11 bankruptcies failed so miserably. Notre Dame Law Review, Volume 68, Issue 1 Article 6. Retrieved April 15, 2019 from https://scholarship.law.nd.edu/cgi/viewcontent.cgi?article=1995&context=ndlr

8.   Warren, E. & Westbrook, J. (2009). The success of Chapter 11: a challenge to the critics. 107 Mich. L. Rev. 603. Retrieved April 15, 2019 from www.researchgate.net/publication/228232563

Lightning Source UK Ltd.
Milton Keynes UK
UKHW042131221021
392564UK00011B/10